Garrett Davis, Alexander Hamilton Stephens

Three Unlike Speeches

by William Lloyd Garrison, of Massachusetts, Garrett Davis, of Kentucky,

Alexander H. Stephens, of Georgia

Garrett Davis, Alexander Hamilton Stephens

Three Unlike Speeches
by William Lloyd Garrison, of Massachusetts, Garrett Davis, of Kentucky, Alexander H. Stephens, of Georgia

ISBN/EAN: 9783337117412

Printed in Europe, USA, Canada, Australia, Japan

Cover: Foto ©ninafisch / pixelio.de

More available books at **www.hansebooks.com**

THE ABOLITIONISTS,

AND THEIR RELATIONS TO THE WAR.

An Address by William Lloyd Garrison, delivered Tuesday Evening, January 14, 1862, at the Cooper Institute, New York. Revised by the Author.

REPORTED BY ANDREW J. GRAHAM.

Among those who occupied the platform were J. A. Kennedy, Superintendent of Police, Rev. Dr. Tyng, Rev. Mr. Sloan, and many other eminent citizens. A beautiful bouquet of flowers and an ivy wreath were placed beside the speaker's desk by Mrs. Paton, which incident was followed by a burst of applause. The speaker having entered, was introduced by Mr. Theodore Tilton, who said:

"LADIES AND GENTLEMEN—I put myself for a moment between you and him [pointing to Mr. Garrison], because I have been asked, and honored in the asking, to give to a genuine Yankee a genuine Yankee welcome; and I know not how to do it better than just to make the old-fashioned sign of the right hand, which is the Yankee token of good fellowship, and in your name to offer it to William Lloyd Garrison." [Applause.]

Mr. Tilton thereupon extended his hand to Mr. Garrison, who forthwith advanced, and was cordially welcomed. Mr. Garrison spoke as follows:

LADIES AND GENTLEMEN: No public speaker, on rising to address an assembly, has any right to presume that, because at the outset he receives a courteous and even warm approval, therefore they are prepared to indorse all his views and utterances. Doubtless, there are some points, at least, about which we very widely differ; and yet, I must frankly confess, I know of no other reason for your kind approval this evening, than that I am an original, uncompromising, irrepressible, out-and-out, unmistakable, Garrisonian Abolitionist. [Enthusiastic applause.] By that designation I do not mean one whose brain is crazed, whose spirit is fanatical, whose purpose is wild and dangerous, but one whose patriotic creed is the Declaration of American Independence [loud cheers], whose moral line of measurement is the Golden Rule, whose gospel of humanity is the Sermon on the Mount, and whose language is that of Ireland's Liberator, O'Connell—"I care not what caste, creed, or color slavery may assume. Whether it be personal or political, mental or corporeal, intellectual or spiritual, I am for its instant, its total abolition. I am for justice, in the name of humanity, and according to the law of the living God." [Cheers.]

Hence, what I wrote many years ago, I feel proud once more to affirm:

"I am an Abolitionist,
 I glory in the name,
Though now by Slavery's minions hissed,
 And covered o'er with shame.
It is a spell of light and power—
 The watchword of the free—
Who spurns it in the trial-hour,
 A craven soul is he."

I know that to be an Abolitionist is not to be with the multitude
—on the side of the majority—in a popular and respectable position; and yet I think I have a right to ask of you, and of all who
are living on the soil of the Empire State, and of the people of the
North at large, why it is that you and they shrink from the name
of Abolitionist? Why is it that, while you profess to be opposed
to slavery, you nevertheless desire the whole world to understand
that you are not radical Abolitionists? What is the meaning of
this? Why are you not all Abolitionists? Your principles are
mine. What you have taught me, I adopt. What you have taken
a solemn oath to support, as essential to a free Government, I
recognize as right and just. The people of this State profess to
believe in the Declaration of Independence. That is my Abolitionism. Every man, therefore, who disclaims Abolitionism,
repudiates the Declaration of Independence. Does he not? "All
men are created equal, and endowed by their Creator with an
inalienable right to liberty." Gentlemen, that is my fanaticism—
that is all my fanaticism. [Cheers.] All I ask is, that this declaration may be carried out everywhere in our country and throughout the world. It belongs to mankind. Your Constitution is an
Abolition Constitution. Your laws are Abolition laws. Your
institutions are Abolition institutions. Your free schools are Abolition schools. I believe in them all; and all that I ask is, that
institutions so good, so free, so noble, may be everywhere propa-
gated, everywhere accepted. And thus it is that I desire, not to
curse the South, or any portion of her people, but to bless her
abundantly, by abolishing her infamous and demoralizing slave
institution, and erecting the temple of liberty on the ruins thereof.

I believe in Democracy; but it is the Democracy which recog-
nizes man as man, the world over. [Cheers.] It is that Democracy which spurns the fetter and the yoke for itself, and for all
wearing the human form. And therefore I say, that any man who
pretends to be a Democrat, and yet defends the act of making
man the property of his fellow-man, is a dissembler and a hypo-
crite, and I unmask him before the universe. [Loud cheers.]

We profess to be Christians. Christianity—its object is to

redeem, not to enslave men! Christ is our Redeemer. I believe in Him. He leads the anti-slavery cause, and always has led it. The Gospel is the Gospel of freedom; and any man claiming to be a Christian, and to have within him the same mind that was in Christ Jesus, and yet dares to hold his fellow-man in bondage, as a mere piece of perishable property, is recreant to all the principles and obligations of Christianity. [Applause.]

Why is it, men of the Empire State, that there are no slaves here? Four millions of people, and not a single slave among them all! On what ground was slavery abolished in the State of New York? On the mere ground of policy or expediency, or because it was an immorality, a crime, an outrage, and therefore not to be tolerated by a civilized and Christian people? Hence I affirm that the people of this State are committed to radical, "ultra" Abolitionism. And so I have a right to expect everywhere a friendly hearing and a warm co-operation on the part of the people when I denounce slavery, and endeavor to bring it to the dust, and to take the chains from those who are laboring under the lash of the slave-driver. You have abolished slavery, because it can have no rightful existence here. You allow no man to decide whether he can humanely hold a slave. So of Massachusetts, so of New England, and so of the nineteen free States. Slavery is pronounced a curse by them all. Every man before the law is equal to every other man; and no man may lay his hand too heavily upon the shoulder of his brother man, except at his peril.

In the very generous notice of this lecture last Sunday, by Henry Ward Beecher, he said that he fully accorded with me in my principles, which strike at the foundation of slavery. All slavery is wrong, unjust, immoral, and unchristian, and ought to terminate, but he expressed some difference of opinion in regard to my methods for its abolition. I am confident that, upon further reflection and investigation, he will find my methods of Abolition are as unexceptionable as my principles. My method is simply this: when I see a slaveholder, I tell him he is bound by every consideration of justice and humanity to let the oppressed go free. That is God's method, and I think there can be no improvement upon it. And when I find an accomplice of the slaveholder sustaining him in his iniquity, I bid him repent, and demand that he bring forth fruits meet for his repentance. That is my method.

Now I say that if we are right in establishing our institutions upon the foundations of equal liberty, we have a right to endeavor to propagate those institutions all over the country and throughout the world. We have a right to say to those in the slave States, " Your system of slavery is inherently wrong and dangerous. Regard your slaves as men, treat them as such, establish free institutions, substitute for the lash a fair compensation, and you will be blest, wonderfully blest." Have I not a right to say this? Is it not a natural, God-given, constitutional right? On the other hand, they have a perfect right at the South to endeavor to proselyte us in regard to their institutions; and I think they have done their best—that is, their worst—in that direction.

I never have heard any complaint in regard to the unlimited freedom of speech on the part of Southern slaveholders and slave-traffickers. We are told by pro-slavery men here, that we have no right to discuss this matter ! They point us to our national compact. They gravely tell us to remember that, at the organization of the Government, the slave States were in existence, and came into the Union on terms of equality, and, under the compact, we have no right to criticise or condemn them because of their holding slaves. Now, my reply to them is, in the first place, that no compact of men's device can bind me to silence when I see my fellow-man unjustly oppressed. [Applause.] I care not when or where the compact was made, or by whom it was approved. My right to denounce tyrants and tyranny is not derived from man, nor from constitutions or compacts. I find it in my own soul, written there by the finger of God, and man can never erase it. I am sure that, if it were your case ; if you were the victims of a compact that denied the right of any one to plead for your deliverance, though you were most grievously oppressed—though your children and wives were for sale in the market, along with cattle and swine—you would exclaim, " Accursed be such a compact ! Let none be dumb in regard to our condition !"

My reply again is, that the compact, bad as it is in its pro-slavery features, provides for the liberty of speech and of the press, and therefore I am justified in saying what I honestly think in regard to slavery and those who uphold it. The Southern slaveholders, I repeat, have always exercised the largest liberty of speech. They have denounced free institutions to an unlimited extent. Is the right all on one side ? May I not reciprocate, and say what I think of their slave institutions? Yes, I have the right, and, by the help of God, I mean to exercise it, come what may. [Great applause.]

The times are changing. Yes, it is spoken of with exultation—

and well it may be as a cheering sign of progress—that even Dr. Brownson has been able to speak against slavery in the city of Washington, without being in peril of his life; that even Horace Greeley and George B. Cheever have been permitted to stand up in the capital of their country, and utter brave words for freedom; and nobody mobbed them! . [Applause.] And I am told it is expected that my eloquent friend, and the friend of all mankind, Wendell Phillips [cheers], will also soon make his appearance at Washington, to be heard on the same subject, without running any great personal risk. This is something to boast of! And yet I must confess, that I feel humiliated when I remember that all this is rendered possible, under our boasted Constitution, only because there is a Northern army of 150,000 soldiers in and around the capital! [Applause.] Take that army away—restore the old state of things—and it would not be possible for such speeches to be made there; but while we have General McClellan and 150,000 Northern bayonets in that section, a Northern man may say aloud at Washington, "Let the Declaration of Independence be applied to all the oppressed in the land," and his life is not specially endangered in so doing! [Cries of "Hear, hear!"] If that is all we have to boast of now, what has been our condition hitherto?

Now, I maintain that no institution has a right to claim exemption from the closest scrutiny. All our Northern institutions are open for inspection. Every man may say of them what he pleases. If he does not like them, he can denounce them. If he thinks he can suggest better ones, he is entitled to do so. Nobody thinks of mobbing him, nobody thinks of throwing rotten eggs and brickbats at his head. Liberty! why, she is always fearless, honest, openhearted. She says, as one did of old, "Search me and try me, and see if there be anything evil in me." But, on the other hand, we are not permitted to examine Southern institutions. Oh, no! And what is the reason? Simply because they will not bear examination! Of course, if the slaveholder felt assured that they could, he would say, "Examine them freely as you will, I will assist you in every way in my power." Ah! "'tis conscience that makes cowards of them all!" They dread the light, and with the tyrant of old they cry, "Put out the light—and then put out the light!" That is their testimony in regard to the rectitude of their slave institutions.

The slaveholders desire to be let alone. Jefferson Davis and his crew cry out, "Let us alone!" The Slave Oligarchy have always

cried out, " Let us alone !" It is an old cry—1,800 years old at
least—it was the cry of those demons who had taken possession of
their victims, and who said to Jesus, " Let us alone! Why hast
thou come to torment us before the time?" [Laughter and applause.] Now, Jesus did not at all mistake the time ; he was precisely
in time, and therefore he bore his testimony like the prince of eman-
cipators, and the foul demons were cast out, but not without rend-
ing the body. The slaves of our country, outraged, lacerated, and
chained, cry out agonizingly to those who are thus treating them,
" Let us alone !"—but the slaveholders give no heed to that cry at
all ! Now, I will agree to let the slaveholders alone when they let
their slaves alone, and not till then. [Applause.]

" Let this matter rest with the South ; leave slavery in the care
and keeping of slaveholders, to put an end to it at the right time,
as they best understand the whole matter." You will hear men,
claiming to be intelligent, talking in this manner continually. They
do not know what idiots they are ; for is it anything better than
idiocy for men to say : " Leave idolatry to idolaters, to be abolished when they think best ; leave intemperance to drunkards ; they
best understand all about it ; they will undoubtedly, if let alone,
in God's own time, put an end to it [laughter] ; leave piracy to be
abolished by pirates ; leave impurity to the licentious to be done
away ; leave the sheep to the considerate humanity of wolves, when
they will cease to prey upon them !" No, this is not common
sense ; it is not sound reason ; it is nothing but sheer folly. Sal-
vation, if it comes at all, must come from without. Those who are
not drunkards must save the drunken ; those who are not impure
must save the impure ; those who are not idolaters must combine
to put down idolatry ; or the world can never make any progress.
So we who are not slaveholders are under obligation to combine,
and by every legitimate method endeavor to abolish slavery ; for
the slaveholders will never do it if they can possibly help it. Why
do you send your missionaries abroad? Why do you go to the isles
of the sea, to Hindostan and Burmah and other parts of the heathen
world with your meddlesome, impertinent, disorganizing religion ?
Because you affirm that your object is good and noble ; because
you believe that the Christian religion is the true religion, and that
idolatry debases and deludes its votaries ; and to abolish it, or to
endeavor to do so, is right. And yet you have no complicity with
heathenism abroad. Nevertheless, your missionaries are there, endeavoring to effect a thorough overturn of all their institutions and

all their established ideas, so that old things shall pass away, and all things become new. But how is it in regard to slavery? You *have* something to do—aye, a great deal to do with it. You ought to know precisely where you stand, and what are your obligations in relation to it. Only think of it! Under your boasted Constitution, two generations of slaves have been driven to unrequited toil, and gone down into bloody graves; and a third generation is going through the same terrible career, with the Star Spangled Banner floating over their heads! This is by your complicity, men of the North! Oh, how consentingly the North has given her sympathy to the South in this iniquity of slaveholding! How everywhere the anti-slavery movement has been spit upon, and denounced, and caricatured, and hunted down, as if it were a wild beast, that could not be tolerated safely for an hour in the community! What weapon has been left unused against the Abolitionists of the North? How thoroughly have the people been tested everywhere, both in Church and State, in relation to the slave system of the South! But "Wisdom is justified of her children." The Abolitionists serenely bide their time. The verdict of posterity is sure; and it will be an honorable acquittal of them from all the foul charges that have been brought against them by a pro-slavery people.

I do not think it is greatly to the shame of Abolitionists that the New York *Herald* can not tolerate them. [Laughter and applause.] I do not think it at all to their discredit that the *Journal of Commerce* thoroughly abominates them. [Laughter.] I do not think they have any cause to hang their heads for shame because the New York *Express* deems them fit only to be spit upon. [Applause.] I do not think they have any reason to distrust the soundness of their religion because the New York *Observer* brands them as infidels. [Applause.] Captain Rynders is not an Abolitionist. [Great laughter.] The Bowery Boys do not like Abolitionism. [Laughter.] And as it was eighteen hundred years ago, so we have had, in this trial of the nation, the chief priests and Scribes and Pharisees on the one hand, and the rabble on the other, endeavoring by lawless means and murderous instrumentalities to put down the anti-slavery movement, which is of God, and can not be put down. [Applause.] The slaveholders who have risen in rebellion to overthrow the Government, and crush out free institutions, are in the mood of mind, and ever have been, to hang every Abolitionist they can catch. I hold that to be a good certificate of character [applause], and when I add that the millions

of slaves in bondage, perishing in their chains, and crying unto
Heaven for deliverance, are ever ready to give their blessings to
the Abolitionists for what they have done, and when they run
away from their masters come to us, who are represented to be
their deadliest enemies, it seems to me we have made out our case.
Such Abolitionism every honest, humane, upright, and noble soul
ought to indorse as right.

And besides, I say it is a shame that we should any longer stand
apart—I mean we of the North. What are all your paltry distinctions worth? You are not Abolitionists. Oh, no. You are only
anti-slavery! Dare you trust yourself in Carolina, except, perhaps,
at Port Royal? [Laughter.] You are not an ultra anti-slavery
man; there is nothing ultra about you. You are only a Republican! Dare you go to New Orleans? Why, the President of the
United States, chosen by the will of the people, and duly inaugu-
rated by solemn oath, is an outlaw in nearly every slave State in
this Union! He can not show himself there, except at the peril
of his life. And so of his Cabinet. I think it is time, under these
circumstances, that we should all hang together, or, as one said of
old, "We shall be pretty sure, if caught, to hang separately."
[Laughter.] The South cares nothing for these nice distinctions
among us. It is precisely on this matter of slavery as it is in
regard to the position of Rome respecting Protestantism. Our
Protestant sects assume to be each one the true sect, as against
every other, and we are free in our denunciation of this or that
sect as heretical, because not accepting our particular theological
creed. What does Rome care for any such distinction? Whether
we are High Church Episcopalian or Methodist, Quaker or Univer-
salist, Presbyterian or Unitarian, we are all included in unbelief,
we are all heretics together; and she makes no compromise. Just
so with slavery. If we avow that we are at all opposed to slavery, it is enough, in the judgment of the South, to condemn us to
a coat of tar and feathers, and to general outlawry.

I come now to consider what are the relations of the Abolitionists to the war. Fourteen months ago, after a heated Presidential
struggle, with three candidates in the field, Abraham Lincoln was
duly and constitutionally chosen President of the United States.
Now where are we? At that time, who doubted the stability of
the American Union? What power in the universe had we to
fear? Was it not pronounced impossible for any real harm to
come to us? How strong was our mountain, and how confident

our expectations in regard to the future! And now our country is dismembered, the Union sundered, and we are in the midst of the greatest civil war that the world has ever known. For a score of years, prophetic voices were heard admonishing the nation, "Because ye have said, We have made a covenant with death, and with hell are we at agreement; when the overflowing scourge shall pass through, it shall not come unto us; for we have made lies our refuge, and under falsehood have we hid ourselves. Therefore, thus saith the Lord God, Judgment will I lay to the line, and righteousness to the plummet; and the waters shall overflow the hiding-place; and your covenant with death shall be annulled, and your agreement with hell shall not stand." And now it is verified to the letter with us. In vain are all efforts to have it otherwise. "He that sitteth in the heavens shall laugh, the Lord shall have them in derision." "Though hand join in hand, yet shall not the wicked go unpunished." Yes, America! "Though thou exalt thyself as the eagle, and though thou set thy nest among the stars, thence will I bring thee down, saith the Lord."

Who are responsible for this war? If I should go out into the streets for a popular reply, it would be, "The Abolitionists"—or, to use the profane vernacular of the vile, "It is all owing to the d—d Abolitionists. [Laughter.] If they had not meddled with the subject of slavery, everything would have gone on well; we should have lived in peace all the days of our lives. But they insisted upon meddling with what doesn't concern them; they indulged in censorious and harsh language against the slaveholders, and the result is, our nation is upturned, and we have immense hostile armies looking each other fiercely in the face, and our glorious Union is violently broken asunder." Let me read an extract from the New York *Express* for your express edification:

"Our convictions are, that anti-slavery stimulated, and is the animating cause of this rebellion. If anti-slavery were now removed from the field of action, pro-slavery would perish of itself, at home, in its own contortions." [Laughter.]

Well, I do not think I can make a better reply to such nonsense than was made by your chairman, in a brief letter which he sent to the annual meeting of the Pennsylvania Anti-Slavery Society at West Chester, a few weeks ago, and by his permission I will read it:

"My opinion is this: There is war because there was a Republican party. There was a Republican party because there was an Abolition party. There was an Abolition party because there was slavery. Now, to charge the war upon Republicanism is merely to blame the lamb that stood in the brook. To charge it upon Abolitionism is merely to blame the sheep for being the lamb's mother. [Laughter.] But to charge it upon slavery is to lay the crime flat at the door of the wolf, where it belongs. [Laughter.] To the end of trouble, kill the wolf. [Renewed laughter.] I belong to the party of wolf-killers." [Applause and merriment.]

And let all the people say Amen! [Cheers.]

But consider the absurdity of this charge. Who are the avowed Abolitionists of our country? I have told you they occupy a very unpopular position in society—and certainly very few men have yet had the moral courage to glory in the name of Abolitionist. They are comparatively a mere handful. And yet they have over-turned the Government! They have been stronger than all the parties and all the religious bodies of the country—stronger than the Church, and stronger than the State. Indeed! Then it must be because with them is the power of God, and it is the Truth which has worked out this marvelous result. [Cheers.]

How many Abolition presses do you suppose exist in this coun-try? We have, I believe, three or four thousand journals printed in the United States; and how many Abolition journals do you suppose there are? [Laughter.] You can count them all by the fin-gers upon your hand; yet, it seems, they are more than a match for all the rest put together. This is very extraordinary; but, our enemies being judges, it is certainly true. And now, what has been our crime? I affirm, before God, that our crime has been only this: we have endeavored, at least, to remember those in bonds as bound with them. I, for one, am guilty only to this extent: I have called aloud for more than thirty years to my beloved but guilty country, saying:

> " There is within thy gates a pest,
> Gold, and a Babylonish vest;
> Not hid in sin-concealing shade,
> But broad against the sun displayed!
> Repent thee, then, and quickly bring
> Forth from the camp th' accursed thing;
> Consign it to remorseless fire,
> Watch till the latest spark expire;
> Then strew its ashes on the wind,
> Nor leave one atom wreck behind.
> So shall thy wealth and power increase;
> So shall thy people dwell in peace;
> On thee th' Almighty's glory rest,
> And all the earth in thee be blest!"

And what if the Abolitionists had been heeded thirty years ago? Would there now be any civil war to talk about? [Cries of " No."] Ten years ago? five years ago? one year ago? And all that time God was patient and forbearing, giving us an opportunity of escape. But the nation would not hearken, and went on hardening its heart. Oh! how guilty are the conspirators of the South in what they have done! How utterly unjustifiable and causeless is their rebel-lion! How foul and false their accusations against the Government,

against the Republican party, against the people of the North !
Utterly, inexcusably, and horribly wicked ! But let us remember,
to our shame and condemnation as a people, that the guilt is not
all theirs. I assert that they have been encouraged in every con-
ceivable way to do all this for more than thirty years—encouraged
by the press of the North, by the churches of the North, by the
pulpits of the North (comprehensively speaking). Abolitionists
have been hunted as outlaws, or denounced as wild fanatics; while
the slaveholders have been encouraged to go on, making one demand after another, until they felt assured that when they struck
this blow, they would have a powerful party at the North with
them, to accomplish their treasonable designs; and it is only by
God's providence we have escaped utter ruin. [Loud applause.]
Therefore it is that the vials of Divine retribution are poured out
so impartially. We are suffering; our blood is flowing, our property is melting away—and who can see the end of it? Well, if
the whole nation should be emptied, I should say : " Oh ! give
thanks unto the Lord ; for he is good, for his mercy endureth forever !" Our crime against these four millions of slaves, and against
a similar number who have been buried, can not be adequately de-
scribed by human language. Our hands are full of blood, and we
have run to do evil ; and now a heavy but righteous judgment is
upon us ! Let us reverently acknowledge the hand of God in this;
let us acknowledge our sins, and put them away ; and let each man
put the trump of jubilee to his lips, and demand that the chains of
the oppressed shall be broken forever ! [Cheers.]

" The Abolitionists have used very irritating language !" I know
it. I think, however, it must be admitted that that charge has
been fully offset by the Southern slaveholders and their Northern
accomplices ; for, if my memory serves me, they have used a great
deal of irritating language about the Abolitionists. Indeed, I do
not know of any abusive, false, profane, malicious, abominable
epithets which they have not applied without stint to the Abolitionists—besides any amount of tarring and feathering, and other
brutal outrages, in which we have never indulged towards them !
[Laughter and cheers.] Irritating language, forsooth ? Why,
gentlemen, all that we have said is, " Do not steal," " Do not mur-
der," " Do not commit adultery."—and it has irritated them ! [Ap-
plause and laughter.] Of course, it must irritate them. The galled
jade will wince. John Hancock and Sam Adams greatly irritated
George the Third and Lord North. There was a great deal of

British irritation at Lexington and Bunker Hill, and it culminated at last at Yorktown. [Loud cheers.] Well, it is certain that a very remarkable change has taken place within a short time. They who have complained of our hard language, as applied to the slaveholders, are now for throwing cannon-balls and bomb-shells at them! They have no objection to blowing out their brains, but you must not use hard language! Now, I would much rather a man would hurl a hard epithet at my head than the softest cannon-ball or shell that can be found in the army of the North. As a people, however, we are coming to the conclusion that, after all, the great body of the slaveholders are not exactly the honest, honorable, and Christian men that we mistook them to be. [Applause.] It is astonishing, when any wrong is done to us, how easily we can see its true nature. What an eye-salvo it is! If any one picks *our* pocket, of course he is a thief; if any one breaks into *our* house, he is a burglar; if any one undertakes to outrage *us*, he is a scoundrel. And now that these slaveholders are in rebellion against the Government, committing piracy upon our commerce, confiscating Northern property to the amount of hundreds of millions of dollars, and plunging the country into all the horrors of civil war, why, of course, they are pirates—they are swindlers—they are traitors of the deepest dye! [Cheers and laughter.] Ladies and gentlemen, let me tell you one thing, and that is, they are just as good as they ever were. They are just as honest, just as honorable, and just as Christian as they ever were. [Laughter.] Circumstances alter cases, you know. While they were robbing four millions of God's despised children of a different complexion from our own, stripping them of all their rights, selling them in lots to suit purchasers, and trafficking in their blood, they were upright, patriotic, Christian gentlemen! Now that they have interfered with us and our rights, have confiscated our property, and are treasonably seeking to establish a rival confederacy, they are downright villains and traitors, who ought to be hanged by the neck until they are dead. [Cheers.]

"Abolitionists should not have intermeddled with their affairs," it is said. "We of the North are not responsible for slavery, and it is a very good rule for men to mind their own business." Who say this? Hypocrites, dissemblers, men who are condemned out of their own mouths. They are those who are always justifying or apologizing for slavery, who are in religious fellowship with these traffickers in human souls, who claim political affinity with them, and who give constitutional guarantees that fugitive slaves may be hunted and captured in every part of the North, and that slave insurrections shall be suppressed by the strong arm of the national Government, if need be; and yet they have nothing to do with slavery! Hypocrites and dissemblers, I spurn you all! When I see a man drowning, if I can throw him a rope, I will do it; and if I would not, would I not be a murderer? When I see a man falling among thieves, and wounded and forsaken, if I can get to him with oil and wine to bind up his wounds, I am bound to do it; and if I refuse, I become as base as the robber who struck him down. And when I see tyranny trampling upon my fellow-man, I know of no law, human or divine, which binds me to silence. I am bound to protest against it. [Cheers.] I will not be dumb. It is my business to meddle with oppression wherever I see it. [Applause.]

It is said, again, " There was no trouble in the land until the Abolitionists appeared." Well, the more is the pity! Order reigns in Warsaw until Kosciusko makes his appearance. It reigns in Hungary until Kossuth comes forward—in Italy, until Garibaldi takes the field. [Loud cheers.] No trouble until the Aboli;i;nists came forward! The charge is false—historically untrue. Witness the struggle that took place at the formation of your Constitution, in regard to the slavery guarantees of that instrument. What is the testimony of John Quincy Adams on that point? He says:

" In the articles of Confederation, there was no guaranty for the property of the slaveholder—no double representation of him in the Federal councils—no power of taxation—no stipulation for the recovery of fugitive slaves. But when the powers of *Government* came to be delegated to the Union, the South—that is, South Carolina and Georgia—refused their subscription to the parchment till it should be saturated with the infection of slavery, which no fumigation could purify, no quarantine could extinguish. The freemen of the North gave way, and the deadly venom of slavery was infused into the Constitution of Freedom."

And so at the time of the Missouri struggle in 1820. There were no Abolitionists then in the field; yet the struggle between freedom and slavery was at that time so fierce and terrible as to threaten to end in a dissolution of the Union. . [Cheers.] Oh! no stain of blood rests on the garments of the Abolitionists. They have endeavored to prevent the awful calamity which has come upon the nation, and they may wash their hands in innocency, and thank God that in the evil day they were able to stand. [Applause.]

No, my friends, this fearful state of things is not of men; it is of Heaven. As we have sowed, we are reaping. The whole cause of it is declared in the memorable verse of the prophet: " Ye have not hearkened unto me in proclaiming liberty, every man to his brother, and every man to his neighbor: behold, I proclaim a liberty for you, saith the Lord, to the sword, to the pestilence, and to the famine." That is the whole story. This is the settlement day of God Almighty for the unparalleled guilt of our nation; and if we desire to be saved, we must see to it that we put away our sins, "break every yoke, and let the oppressed go free," and thus save our land from ruin. [Applause.]

Be not deceived; this rebellion is not only to eternize the enslavement of the African race, but it is also to overturn the free institutions of the North. The slaveholders of the South are not only opposed to Northern Abolitionists, but to Northern ideas and Northern institutions. Shall I refresh your memories by one or two quotations in point? Listen to the language of the Richmond *Examiner:*

"The South now maintains that slavery is right, natural, and necessary, and does not depend upon complexion. The laws of the slave States justify the holding of *white men* in bondage."

The Charleston *Mercury* says:

"Slavery is the natural and normal condition of the laboring man, whether white or black. The great evil of Northern free (mark you, not *Abolition*) society is that it is burdened with a servile class, mechanics and laborers, unfit for self-government, and yet clothed with the attributes and powers of citizens. Master and slave is a relation in society as necessary as that of parent and child; and the Northern States will yet have to introduce it. *Their theory of free government is a delusion.'*

Yet you are for free government, but not for Abolitionism! What do you gain by the disclaimer? The South is as much opposed to the one as she is to the other—she hates and repudiates them both!

The Richmond *Enquirer* says:

"Two opposite and conflicting forms of society can not, among civilized men, co-exist and endure. The one must give way and cease to exist. The other becomes universal. If free society be unnatural, immoral, unchristian, it must fall, and give way to slave society—a social system old as the world, universal as man."

An Alabama paper says:

"All the Northern, and especially the New England States, are devoid of society fitted for well-bred gentlemen. The prevailing class one meets with is that of mechanics struggling to be genteel, and small farmers who do their own drudgery, and yet who are hardly fit for associating with a Southern gentleman's body-servant."

You see, men of the North, it is a war against freedom—your freedom as well as that of the slave—against the freedom of mankind. It is to establish an oligarchic, slaveholding despotism, to the extinction of all free institutions. The Southern rebellion is in full blast; and if they can work their will against us, there will be for us no liberty of speech or of the press—no right to assemble as we assemble here to-night, and our manhood will be trampled in the dust. [Applause.] I say, therefore, under these circumstances, treason consists in giving aid or countenance to the slave system of the South—not merely to Jeff Davis, as president of the Southern Confederacy, or to this rebel movement in special. Every man who gives any countenance or support to slavery is a traitor to liberty. [Enthusiastic applause.] I say he is a dangerous and unsafe man. [Renewed cheers.] He carries within him the seeds of despotism, and no one can tell how soon a harvest of blood and treason may spring up. Liberty goes with Union and for Union, based on judgment and equality. Slavery is utter disunion and disorganization in God's universe. [Cheers.]

But, we are told, "hang the Secessionists on the one hand, and the Abolitionists on the other, and then we shall have peace." [Laughter.] How very discriminating! Now, I say, if any hanging is to be done (though I do not believe in capital punishment—that is one of my heresies)—if any hanging is to be done, I am for hanging these sneaking, two-faced, pseudo-loyal go-betweens immediately. [Loud and enthusiastic applause. A voice, "That's the talk!"] Why, as to this matter of loyalty, I maintain that the most loyal people to a free government who walk on the American soil, are the uncompromising Abolitionists. [Cheers.] It is not freedom that rises in rebellion against free government. It is not the love of liberty that endangers it. It is not those who will not make any compromise with tyranny who threaten it. It is those who strike hands with the oppressors. Yes, I maintain the Abolitionists are more loyal to free government and free institutions than President Lincoln himself; because, while I want to say everything good of him that I can, I must say I think he is lacking somewhat in backbone, and is disposed, at least, to make some compromise with slavery, in order to bring back the old state of things; and, therefore, he is nearer Jeff Davis than I am. Still, we are both so bad, that I suppose if we should go amicably together down South, we never should come back again.

"Hang the Abolitionists, and then hang the Secessionists!" Why, in the name of common sense, wherein are these parties agreed? Their principles and purposes are totally dissimilar. *We* believe in the inalienable rights of man—in "liberty, equality, fraternity." *They* disbelieve in all these. *We* believe in making the law of God paramount to all human codes, compacts, and enactments. *They* believe in trampling it under their feet, to gratify their lust of dominion, and in "exalting themselves above all that is called God." *We* believe in the duty of liberating all who are pining in bondage. *They* are for extending and perpetuating slavery to the latest posterity. *We* believe in free government and free institutions. *They* believe in the overthrow of all these, and have made chattel bondage the corner-stone of their new confederacy. Where is there any agreement or similarity between these parties?

But it may be said you are for the dissolution of the Union. I was. Did I have any sympathy with the spirit of Southern secession when I took that position? No. My issue was a moral one—a Christian one. It was because of the pro-slavery nature of the compact itself that I said I could not, as a Christian man, as a friend of liberty, swear to uphold such a Union or Constitution. Listen to the declaration of John Quincy Adams, a most competent witness, I think, in regard to this matter:

"It can not be denied—the slaveholding lords of the South prescribed as a condition of their assent to the Constitution, three specific provisions to secure the perpetuity of their dominion over their slaves. The first was the immunity for twenty years of preserving the slave-trade; the second was the stipulation to surrender fugitive slaves—an engagement positively prohibited by the laws of God, delivered from Sinai ; and thirdly, the exaction, fatal to the principles of popular representation, of a representation of slaves, for articles of merchandise, under the name of persons.

"The bargain between freedom and slavery, contained in the Constitution of the United States, is *morally and politically vicious*—inconsistent with the principles on which alone our Revolution can be jus ified—cruel and oppressive, by riveting the chains of slavery, by pledging the faith of freedom to maintain and perpetuate the tyranny of the master, and grossly unequal and impolitic, by admitting that slaves are at once enemies to be kept in subjection, property to be secured and returned to their owners, and persons not to be represented themselves, but for whom their masters are privileged with nearly a double share of representation. The consequence has been that this slave represcontation has governed the Union. Benjamin's portion above his brethren has ravined as a wolf. In the morning he has devoured the prey, and in the evening has divided the spoil."

Hence I adopted the language of the prophet Isaiah, and pronounced the Constitution, in these particulars, to be " a covenant with death, and an agreement with hell." Was I not justified as a Christian man in so doing? Oh, but the New York *Journal of Commerce* says there seems to have taken place a great and sudden change in my views—I no longer place this motto at the head of my paper. Well, ladies and gentlemen, you remember what Benedick in the play says : " When I said I would die a bachelor, I did not think I would live to get married." [Laughter.] And when I said I would not sustain the Constitution, because it was " a covenant with death, and an agreement with hell," *I had no idea that I would live to see death and hell secede.* [Prolonged applause and laughter.] Hence it is that I am now with the Government to enable it to constitutionally stop the further ravages of death, and to extinguish the flames of hell forever. [Renewed applause.]

We are coolly told that slavery has nothing to do with this war! Believe me, of all traitors in this country who are most to be feared and detested, they are those who raise this cry. We have little to fear, I think, from the Southern rebels, comparatively : it is those Northern traitors, who, under the mask of loyalty, are doing the work of the devil, and effectively aiding the Secessionists by trying to intimidate the national government from striking a direct blow at the source of the rebellion, who make our position a dangerous one. [Applause.] What? slavery nothing to do with this war! How does it happen, then, that the war is all along the border between the free and the slave States? What is the meaning of this? For there is not a truly loyal slave State in the Union—not one. [Voices—"That's so."] I maintain that Maryland, Kentucky, and Missouri are, by their feigned loyalty, greater obstacles in the way of victory than Carolina, Alabama, and Georgia. Nothing but the presence on their soil of the great army of the North keeps them loyal, even in form, and even under such a pressure they are full of overt treason. They have to be enticed to remain in the Union, as a man said he once enticed a burglar out of his house—he enticed him with a pitchfork! [Laughter.] Withdraw your troops, and instantly they will fall into the Southern Confederacy by the law of gravitation. That is the whole of it. But this is not to be loyal—this is not a willing support of the Constitution and the Union. No! On the other hand, every free State is true to the Government. It is the inevitable struggle between the children of the bond-woman and the children of the free. [Applause.]

Treason—where is it most rampant? Just where there are the most slaves! It disappears where there are no slaves, except in those cases to which I have referred, of skulking, double-faced hypocrites, wearing the mask of loyalty, and yet having the heart of traitors. [Applause.] What State led off in this atrocious rebellion? Why, South Carolina, of course, for in that State the slave population outnumbers the white. And so of Louisiana, out of which every avowed Unionist has been driven by violence: more than half of her population are slaves. Charleston and New Orleans are the head-quarters of treason, because the head-quarters of slavery. Besides, do not the rebels proclaim to the world that the issue they make is the perpetuation of their slave system and the overthrow of free government? Commend them for their openness: they avow just what they mean, and what they desire to accomplish. Now, then, for any party at the North to say, "Don't point at slavery as the source of the rebellion—it has nothing whatever to do with it—the Abolitionists are alone to be held responsible"—why, I have no words to express my contempt for such dissemblers. I brand them as worse than the rebels who are armed and equipped for the seizure of the capital.

It is loudly vociferated in certain quarters, "This is not a war for the abolition of slavery, but solely to maintain the Union." Granted, ten thousand times over! I, as an Abolitionist, have never asserted the contrary. But the true issue is, in order that the Union may be perpetuated, shall not slavery, the cause of its dismemberment, be stricken down to the earth? The necessity is found in the present imperiled state of the Government, and in the fatal experiment of the past. There can not again be a union of the States as it existed before the rebellion; for while I will not underrate Northern valor, but believe that Northern soldiers are competent to achieve anything that men can do in the nature of things, I have no faith in the success of the army in its attempt to subdue the South, while leaving slavery alive upon her soil. If any quarter is given to it, it seems to me that our defeat is just as certain in the end as that God reigns. We have got to make up our minds to one of three alternatives; either to be vanquished by the rebel forces, or to see the Southern Confederacy shortly acknowledged by the European powers: or else, for self-preservation and to maintain its supremacy over the whole country, the Government must transform every slave into a man and a freeman, henceforth to be protected as such under the national ensign. [Applause.] The right of the Government to do this, in the present fearful emergency, is unquestionable. Has not slavery made itself an outlaw? And what claim has an outlaw upon the Constitution or the Union? Guilty of the blackest treason, what claims have the traitors upon the Government? Why, the claim to be hanged by the neck until they are "dead, dead, dead"—nothing else. [Applause.]

What sane man, what true patriot, wants the old Union restored —the Slave Oligarchy once more in power over the free States— Congress under slaveholding mastership—the army, navy, treasury, executive, supreme court, all controlled by the traffickers in human flesh? No! no! Happily, the Government may now constitutionally do what until the secession it had not the power to do. For thirty years the Abolitionists have sent in their petitions to Congress, asking that body to abolish slavery in the District of Columbia, to prevent the further extension of slavery, to repeal the Fugitive Slave Law, etc., etc., but not to interfere with slavery in the Southern States. We recognize the compact as it was made. But now, by their treasonable course, the slaveholders may no longer demand constitutional protection for their slave property. The old "covenant with death" should never have been made. Our fathers sinned—sinned grievously and inexcusably—when they consented to the hunting of fugitive slaves—to a slave representation in Congress—to the prosecution of the foreign slave-trade, under the national flag, for twenty years—to the suppression of slave insurrections by the whole power of the Government. I know the dire extremity in which they were placed—exhausted by a seven years' war, reduced to bankruptcy, bleeding at every pore, fearing that the colonies would be conquered in detail by England if they did not unite—it was a terrible temptation to compromise; but it does not exonerate them from guilt. The Union should not have been made upon such conditions; but now that the South has trampled it under foot, it must not be restored as it was, even if it can be done. [Applause.] But it can not be done. There are two parties who will make such a reunion impossible: the first is, the South— the second, the North. Besides, what reliable guarantee could be given that, after coming back, the South would not secede within twenty-four hours? The right to secede *ad libitum* is her cardinal doctrine. Moreover, she declares that she has taken her leave of us forever; she will not unite with us on any terms. Let me read you an extract from Jefferson Davis's last message to the Confederate Congress:

"Not only do the causes which induced us to separate still last in full force, but they have been strengthened; and whatever doubt may have lingered on the minds of any, must have been completely dispelled by subsequent events. If, instead of being a dissolution of a league, it were indeed a rebellion in which we are engaged, we might feel ample vindication for the course we have adopted in the scenes which are now being enacted in the United States. Our people now look with contemptuous astonishment on those with whom they have been so recently associated. They shrink with aversion from the bare idea of renewing such a connection. With such a people we may be content to live at peace, but *our separation is final*, and for the independence we have asserted we will accept no alternative."

Now, this is open and above-board, and it ought to be resolutely met by the North in the glorious spirit of freedom, saying, "By the traitorous position you have assumed, you have put your slave system under the absolute control of the Government; and that you may be saved from destruction, as well as the country, we shall emancipate every slave in your possession." [Cheers.]

But—say the sham loyalists of the North, "there is no constitutional right or power to abolish slavery—it would be the overthrow of the Constitution if Congress or the President should dare to do it." This is nothing better than cant, and treason in disguise. I should like to know what right General McClellan has with an invading army of 150,000 men in Virginia? Is that constitutional? Did Virginia bargain' for that when she entered the Union? By what right did we batter down the fort at Cape Hatteras? By what right do Northern soldiers "desecrate the sacred soil" of South Carolina by capturing Port Royal and occupying Beaufort? By what right has the Government half a million of troops, invading the South in every quarter, to kill, slay, and destroy, to "cry havoc, and let slip the dogs of war," for the purpose of bringing her into subjection? Where is the right to do this to be found in the Constitution? Where is it? It is in this section : " CONGRESS SHALL HAVE POWER TO DECLARE WAR;" and when war comes, then come the rules of war, and, UNDER THE WAR POWER, Congress has a constitutional right to abolish slavery if it be necessary to save the Government and maintain the Union. [Loud applause.] On this point, what better authority do we want than that of John Quincy Adams? Hear what he says:

" I lay this down as the law of nations. I say that military authority takes, for the time, the place of all municipal institutions, and *slavery among the rest;* and that under that state of things, so far from its being true that the States where slavery exists have the exclusive management of the subject, not only the President of the United States, but the commander of the army, *has power to order the universal emancipation of the slaves.* * * * From the instant that the slaveholding States become the theater of a war, civil, servile, or foreign, from that instant the war powers of Congress extend to interference with the institution of slavery, in every way in which it can be interfered with, from a claim of indemnity for slaves taken or destroyed, to the cession of States, burdened with slavery, to a foreign power. * * * It is a war power. I say it is a war power; and when your country is actually in war, whether it be a war of invasion or a war of insurrection, Congress has power to carry on the war, and must carry it on, according to the laws of war; and by the laws of war, an invaded country has all its laws and municipal institutions swept by the board, and martial power takes the place of them. When two hostile armies are set in martial array, the commanders of both armies *have power to emancipate all the slaves in the invaded territory.*"

I hope Gen. McClellan or President Lincoln will soon be inclined to say "ditto" to John Quincy Adams. [Applause.] Commander-in-chief of the army, by the law of nations and under the war power given by the Constitution, in this terrible emergency you have the right and glorious privilege to be the great deliverer of the millions in bondage, and the savior of your country! May you have the spirit to do it!

There are some well-meaning men who unreflectingly say that this is despotic power. But the exercise of a constitutional right is not despotism. What the people have provided to save the Government or the Union is not despotism, but the concentration of extraordinary power for beneficent purposes. It is as much a constitutional act, therefore, for Gen. McClellan, or the President, or Congress, to declare slavery at an end in this country, as it is to march an army down into the South to subdue her—as it is to give shelter and freedom to the thousands of contrabands already set at liberty. The way is clear; and under these circumstances, how tremendous will be the guilt of the Government if it refuses to improve this marvelous opportunity to do a magnificent work of justice to one seventh portion of our whole population—to do no evil to the South, but to bestow upon her a priceless blessing, and thereby perpetuate all that is precious in our free institutions! I would rather take my chance at the judgment-seat of God with Pharaoh than with Abraham Lincoln if he do not, as President of the United States, in this solemn exigency, let the people go. [Applause.] He has the power—he has the right. The capital is virtually in a state of siege—the rebels are strong, confident, defiant; scarcely any progress has been made in quelling the rebellion. We do not know where we are, or what is before us. Already hundreds of millions of dollars in debt—blood flowing freely, but in vain—the danger of the speedy recognition of the Southern Confederacy by European powers imminent—what valid excuse can the Government give for hesitating under such a pressure? And when you consider that slavery—which in itself is full of weakness and danger to the South—is, by the forbearance of the Government, made a formidable power in the hands of the rebels for its overthrow, you perceive there is a pressing reason why there should be no delay.

Only think of it! Our colored population, bond and free, could furnish an army of a million men from eighteen to forty-five years of age, and yet not one of them is allowed to shoulder a musket! There are in slavery more than eight hundred thousand men capable of bearing arms—a number larger than the two great hostile armies already in the field. They are at the service of the Government whenever it will accept them as free and loyal inhabitants. [Applause.] It will not accept them! But the rebel slaveholders are mustering them in companies and regiments, and they are shooting down Northern men, and in every way giving strength and success to the rebellion. Slavery is a thunderbolt in the hands of the traitors to smite the Government to the dust. That thunderbolt might be seized and turned against the rebellion with fatal effect, and at the same time without injury to the South. My heart glows when I think of the good thus to be done to the oppressors as well as to the oppressed; for I could not stand here, I could not stand anywhere, and advocate vindictive and destructive measures to bring the rebels to terms. I do not believe in killing or doing injury even to enemies—God forbid! That is not my Christian philosophy. But I do say, that never before in the history of the world has God vouchsafed to a government the power to do such a work of philanthropy and justice, in the extremity of its danger and for self preservation, as he now grants to this Government. Emancipation is to destroy nothing but evil; it is to establish good; it is to transform human beings from things into men; it is to make freedom, and education, and invention, and enterprise, and prosperity, and peace, and a true Union possible and sure. Redeemed from the curse of slavery, the South shall in due time be as the garden of God, Though driven to the wall and reduced to great extremity by this rebellion, still we hold off, hold off, and reluctantly say, at last, if it must be so, but only to save ourselves from destruction, we will do this rebellious South the most beneficent act that any people ever yet did—one that will secure historic renown for the administration, make this struggle memorable in all ages, and bring down upon the land the benediction of God! But we will not do this, if we can possibly avoid it! Now, for myself, both as an act of justice to the oppressed and to serve the cause of freedom universally, I want the Government to be in haste to blow the trump of jubilee. I desire to bless and not curse the South—to make her prosperous and happy by substituting free institutions for her leprous system of slavery. I am as much interested in the safety and welfare of the slaveholders, as brother men, as I am in the liberation of their poor slaves; for we are all the children of God, and should strive to promote the happiness of all. I desire that the mission of Jesus, " Peace on earth, good-will to men," may be fulfilled in this and in every land.

Bear in mind that the colored people have always been loyal to the country. You never heard of a traitor among them, when left to freedom of choice. Is it not most humiliating—ought we not to blush for shame—when we remember what we have done to them, and what they have done for us? In our Revolutionary struggle they freely participated, and helped to win our national independence. The first patriotic blood that stained the pavements of Boston, in 1770, was that of Crispus Attucks, a black man. It was Peter Salem, a black man, who shot the British leader, Major Pitcairn, as, storming the breastworks at Bunker Hill, he exclaimed, " The day is ours!" Throughout that memorable struggle, the colored men were ever ready to pour out their blood and lay down their lives to secure the liberties we now enjoy; and they were admitted to have been among the bravest of the brave. In the war of 1812, when New Orleans was threatened by a formidable British force, do you remember what Gen. Jackson said when he needed their help? He did not scorn them in the hour of peril; far from it. This was his proclamation :

" HEADQUARTERS, SEVENTH MILITARY DISTRICT,
MOBILE, *Sept.* 21, 1814.

To the Free Colored Inhabitants of Louisiana :

Through a mistaken policy, you have been heretofore deprived of a participation in the glorious struggle for national rights in which this country in engaged. This no longer shall exist.

As sons of freedom, you are now called upon to defend our most inestimable blessings. As Americans, your country looks with confidence to her adopted children for a valorous support, as a faithful return for the advantages enjoyed under her mild and equitable Government. As fathers, husbands, and brothers, you are summoned to rally round the standard of the eagle, to defend all which is dear in existence.

Your country, although calling for your exertions, does not wish you to engage in her cause without remunerating you for the services rendered. Your intelligent minds are not to be led away by false representations. Your love of honor would cause you to despise the man who should attempt to deceive you. With the sincerity of a soldier and the language of truth I address you.

To every noble-hearted freeman of color volunteering to serve during the present contest with Great Britain, and no longer, there will be paid the same bounty, in money and lands, now received by the white soldiers of the United States, viz.: one hundred and twenty-four dollars in money, and one hundred and sixty acres of land. The non-commissioned officers and privates will also be entitled to the same monthly pay, daily rations, and clothes furnished to any American soldier.

As a distinct, independent battalion or regiment, pursuing the path of glory, you will, undivided, receive the applause and gratitude of your countrymen."

Then again, after the struggle, he addressed them as follows:

" Soldiers! When, on the banks of the Mobile, I called upon you to take up arms, inviting you to partake of the perils and glory of your white fellow-citizens, I expected much from you ; for I was not ignorant that you possessed qualities most formidable to an invading enemy. I knew with what fortitude you could overcome hunger and thirst, and all the fatigues of a campaign. *I knew well how you loved your native country*, and that you, as well as ourselves, had to defend what man holds most dear—his parents, wife, children, and property. *You have done more than I expected.* In addition to the previous qualities I before knew you to possess, I have found among you a noble enthusiasm, which leads to the performance of great things."

What a splendid tribute!—" I expected much from you, but you have done more than I expected!"

I do not believe in war, but I do say that, if any class of men, being grievously oppressed, ever had the right to seize deadly weapons, and smite their oppressors to the dust, then all men have the same right. [Applause.]   " A man 's a man, for a' that."   If the right of bloody resistance is in proportion to the amount of oppression inflicted, then no people living would be so justified before heaven and earth in resisting unto blood as the Southern slaves. By that rule, any Nat Turner has a right to parody the famous Marseillaise, and, addressing his suffering associates, exclaim—

" Ye lettered slaves! awake to glory!
Hark ! hark ! what myriads bid you rise!
Your children, wives, and grandsires ho ry,
Behold their tears and hear their cries!
To arms, to arms, ye brave !
The patriot sword unsheath !
March on, march on, all hearts resolved
On liberty or death!"

Thus do I vindicate the equal humanity of the slaves. Let them be emancipated under law as the flag of the Union goes forward, and they will behave as well as any other class. They are not a bloodthirsty race; they are calumniators who make this charge. The Anglo-Saxon race are far more vindictive and revengeful ; but the African race are peculiarly mild, gentle, forbearing, forgiving. So much indeed do they dread to shed blood, that they can not successfully conspire to throw off the yoke without some one of them who has been treated kindly, and who desires to shield his master or mistress from harm, reveals the secret ! When they are set f ee and protected as free men by the Government, there will be little need of a Northern army at the South ; for they will take care of the rebel slaveholders, and the rebellion with speedily collapse. [Applause.]

It is further said, by way of intimidation, that if the Government proclaim emancipation, a large portion of the officers in the army will instantly resign, and the army itself be broken up. Then they will be guilty of treason. [A voice—" They ought to be hanged."]

If such are the officers and such the soldiers, then the army is filled with traitors. But I believe the imputation to be as false as the prediction is intended to be mischievous.

There is no squeamishness at the South, on the part of the rebels, in making use of the slaves to carry on their treasonable purposes. They are used in every way, not merely to provide food and raise cotton, but to make rifle-pits, construct batteries, and perform military service. There are two regiments of black soldiers at Centreville, with more than a thousand man each, compelled to engage in the work of butchering those who are loyal to the Union! Yet the Government can have them all any hour it chooses to insure their liberty. Refusing to do this, is not the Government itself practically guilty of treason to that extent, and making its overthrow doubly sure? This is a serious inquiry, and it ought to be answered in a serious manner.

The worst traitors are those who claim an exemption for the rebels from loss of slave property, which the rebels themselves do not demand. I turn to the latter, and ask, "Do you claim anything of us?" "Nothing, except to hate and spurn you." "Do you claim anything of the Constitution?" "Nothing, except the right to trample it beneath our feet." "Do you deny that we have a right to abolish slavery, if we can, since you have treasonably withdrawn from the Union?" "No—we do not deny it; we counted the cost of secession, and took all the risk; you have not only the right, as a war power, to liberate every slave in our possession, but [aside], if you are not idiots, you will do so without delay." What if they had a similar advantage on their side? What if there were eight hundred thousand men at the North, qualified to bear arms, who at a signal could be made to co-operate for the triumph of secession? Do you suppose they would allow such an opportunity to pass unimproved for one moment? If they do not pretend to have any rights under the old Constitution, are they not more to be detested than the rebels who, here at the North, still insist that they have forfeited none of their rights as slaveholders under that instrument?

This struggle can be happily terminated only in one way—by putting "FREEDOM FOR ALL" on our banner. We may then challenge and shall receive the admiration and support of the civilized world. We shall not then be in any danger from abroad. No—although England has seemed to be hot, and combative, and inclining southward; although the English Government has taken us at disadvantage, with a menacing aspect, in the Mason and Slidell affair; and although the London *Times* and other venal presses, bribed with secession gold, have indulged in contemptuous and bullying language toward the American Government, yet I think I know something of the English heart—and I hesitate not to say that, in spite of all these unfriendly demonstrations, the heart of the English people, the bone and muscle and moral force of the nation, beats sympathizingly with the North rather than with the South [applause]; though we have not secured that sympathy to the full extent, because of the manner in which we have dealt with the slavery question. I will venture to say that any Northern man, intelligent and qualified to address a public assembly, may travel from " the Land's End to John o' Groat's House, and wherever he shall meet a popular assembly, and fairly present the issue now pending before them, so that they can understand it, he will " bring down the house" overwhelmingly in support of the Government, and against the traitorous Secessionists. [Loud applause.]

Shall I refer to one representative man of the middle classes, John Bright [reiterated and long-continued applause], whose recent masterly analysis of this tangled American question, before his constituents at Rochdale, will brighten his name and fame as the discriminating, fearless, and eloquent champion of freedom at home and abroad? He represents the people of England, in the best meaning of that word. Richard Cobden, too, stands by his side, and renders the same enlightened verdict. [Applause.] And on that side of the Atlantic, there is not a more firm, faithful, and earnest supporter of this Government, in its struggle to uphold the Democratic theory, and to put down the tory sentiment of the South—for slavery is toryism run to seed—than the calumniated but eloquent and peerless advocate of negro emancipation, George Thompson. [Cheers.]

Ladies and gentlemen, I thank you a thousand times over for your patient indulgence in so protracted a speech, and for the approval you have bestowed upon my sentiments. We will go forward in the name of God, in the spirit of liberty, determined to have a country, and a whole country—a Constitution, and a free Constitution—a Union, and a just and glorious Union, that shall endure to the latest posterity; and when we shall see this civil war ended, every bondman set free, and universal liberty prevailing from the Atlantic to the Pacific, we may exultingly repeat the language of one* who, in his youthful days, seemed to have the flame of liberty brightly burning in his soul:

"Then hail the day when o'er our land
　　The sun of freedom shone;
When, dimmed and sunk in Eastern skies,
　　He rose upon our own,
To chase the night of slavery,
And wake the slumbering free!
May his light shine more bright,
　　May his orb roll sublime,
　　Till it warm every clime,
And illume from sea to sea!"　　　　　[Applause.]

---

* Caleb Cushing.

THE WAR:

NOT FOR EMANCIPATION OR CONFISCATION.

A Speech by Hon. Garrett Davis, of Kentucky, delivered in the U. S. Senate,
January 23, 1862. Revised by the Author.

Mr. DAVIS commenced speaking on the 22d, upon a resolution expelling Senator Bright, of Indiana, but gave way for the Senate to go into executive session. On the 23d he finished his very able argument on the resolution, and concluded by dealing with the subject of emancipation in reply to several Senators, among whom were Mr. Sumner, of Massachusetts, and Mr. Harlan, of Iowa, to whom it will be noticed he makes allusion. After introducing the subject, and paying a high tribute to John Quincy Adams, he spoke as follows:

I AM for putting down this rebellion. I am for visiting the leaders with every punishment that can be constitutionally inflicted. So far as you can hang the leaders, I say, in the name of justice and of our country, hang them. So far as you can constitutionally forfeit their property—and forfeiting and confiscation are different things—forfeit it. In confiscation, the property goes into the king's exchequer. In forfeiture, it may go to the king, and will go to him, unless there is a different destination expressed; or it may go to the public, or it may go to individuals. I say forfeit all the estate you can constitutionally of those who have taken an active part in this rebellion; and instead of vesting it in the nation —in the United States, if that is disagreeable to gentlemen—forfeit it to the innocent and true and faithful men who have been impoverished, and whose families have been reduced to penury and want by the ravages of this war. Let it make atonement to them. There is a just retribution—in my judgment a constitutional retribution. Let that retribution be made. You may make it in that form without any violation of the Constitution.

At this point let me put a question to the Senator from Massachusetts. While that assembly of sages and of patriots were deliberating upon the formation of the Constitution at Philadelphia, they despaired at one time of being able to accomplish anything, and were about to separate in despair and give up their country in hopeless despondency. Franklin advised that they should appeal to the throne of grace for instruction and light. That appeal was made, and the fruits were afterward manifested in the adoption of the Constitution. Suppose that any member of that convention had proposed to incorporate into the Constitution, in explicit words, just the powers for which the gentleman now contends, how many votes in the convention would such a constitution have obtained? If it could have passed that ordeal, and had come to be submitted, as it was directed and advised by the members of the convention to be submitted, to the people of the States in convention (not in their State government, not to their legislatures, but to the people of the States in their power and capacity, sitting in sovereign convention), how many of the States would have approved of a constitution containing express provisions granting the powers which the gentleman now claims? The Constitution never would have been made.

A few more words, Mr. President, and I have done, and I make my humble apology to the Senate for having detained it so long. The gentleman said that slavery was the cause of this rebellion. In my judgment it has many causes. If the word "slavery" had never been spoken in the halls of Congress, there would have been no rebellion, as I think. One of the remote causes of this rebellion was the acquisition of Texas. I chanced to be a member of the other House when the joint resolution usurping the treaty-making power was introduced in the House of Representatives to admit Texas as a State into the Union. A treaty had been negotiated to that effect a few weeks before by Mr. Calhoun, as secretary of state for Mr. Tyler. The Democratic party, though they wanted to use Tyler to subvert and overthrow the party which placed him in power, never intended to make him their chief, and themselves never confided any power to him. They determined that he and his administration should never have the Jeffersonian glory and fame of having added such a province as Texas to the United States of America.

They therefore voted down that treaty; they would not allow it to get a two-third vote in the Senate, which was requisite. In a few weeks afterward a joint resolution, admitting Texas, a foreign territory, into the Union, was introduced. I say that no constitution was ever more palpably and flagitiously violated than was the Constitution of the United States by the introduction and passage of that resolution. It is preposterous and absurd to say that Congress, the legislative department of the Government, clothed with no part or parcel of the treaty-making power, may admit foreign territory into the United States either as Territory or State. I voted against it then. It is no precedent to me now. It is such a monstrous absurdity that I would not give the act the least consideration if a parallel proposition were now to be offered.

What were the fruits of the annexation of Texas? I allude to that to show how the woof of vice and of crime is interwoven, and how it progresses. Mexico took exception to that act, and she marched her army to Corpus Christi, and under Polk's administration that army was met at Palo Alto and at Resaca de la Palma, by that old son of Mars, Zachary Taylor, and it was overthrown. What did Polk do? He sent a message to Congress declaring that American blood had been shed upon American soil, and asking Congress to repel the invasion. It is a historical and a geographical fact, as demonstrable as such facts can be, that Corpus Christi never had been any part of Texas until it was usurped after the battle of San Jacinto; that when Texas was one of the Mexican states, and one of the Spanish provinces, it had never been any part of Texas. What did Congress do? It recognized the war. I voted against the war, and I denounced the position of the President that American blood had been shed upon American soil as a falsehood; and I think that I conclusively proved it to be so in a speech that I made upon the subject in the House of Representatives. What then took place? As a continuation of that line of policy, I say, came the war with Mexico. I voted against recognizing that war. I voted against it not only for the reason I have stated, but for another reason. I knew that the result of the war would be the acquisition of more territory; and that whenever we got more territory, this apple of discord, this perpetual, this accursed question of negro slavery would again be thrown in to divide and to distract the people. I then went out of Congress, and now have returned. If I had been present in 1821 I might have voted against the Missouri compromise; it is probable I should have done so; but after it had been passed, and had given peace and quiet to the land for a generation, I was utterly opposed to its disturbance; and if I had been a member of either House of Congress in 1854, I should have voted, and I should have exerted myself to preserve that compromise inviolate. When Kansas was sought to be admitted, and the Lecompton constitution was pressed upon Congress for adoption, I investigated the subject, and I admitted and believed and said publicly and boldly that it was a most outrageous and palpable fraud; and if I had been here in 1858 I should have voted against the admission of Kansas under the Lecompton constitution.

Mr. President, I am here as the humblest member of this body;

but I am here not as a factionist, not as a party man. I belong to
no party. I am too old; my remaining years on earth are too few
for me ever to expect to wear another party collar. I am here to
vote, and to do what I deem to be right upon every question, upon
every measure, as it comes up in this House, according to the
lights of my information and of my reason. I am utterly opposed to this emancipation. Oh! in the name of our country, as
gentlemen hope to restore this Union, to crush out this rebellion,
to bring the traitors to justice and to condign punishment, let them
suspend until that consummation any policy or measures which
introduce discord. Until this war closes in triumphant success, in
the glorious reconstruction of the Union, in the assertion of the
majesty of the Constitution and the laws, let us have unity and
peace among all men who want to bring about these results.

I was pained, and inexpressibly pained, the other day, when my
new but most respected friend from Iowa (Mr. Harlan) signified
his willingness to put arms in the hands of the slaves. When that
is done, I would say to my friend that all hope of the reconstruction of this Union is gone—gone forever. Oh! you do not know
what horrors such a measure might produce. Recur to your early
reading; examine again in our Library the history of the insurrection in San Domingo, with all its blood and atrocities, the reading
of which makes human nature shudder. I have seen men refugees
from the servile insurrection of San Domingo, and the living,
glowing, horrid colors in which they painted those scenes to me,
haunt my memory to this day. Read the accounts of the alarm
produced in Richmond many, many years ago by the meditated
insurrection by the slave Gabriel; trace the limited, but bloody
and frightful course of the more recent servile revolt in South-
ampton. But a few days since, when England seemed to choose
this time of our division and civil war to pick a quarrel with us,
both the mother country and Canada sent out a rally cry to the
fugitive slaves in her provinces to form themselves into companies
and regiments to take part in a war against this country, in invading the United States, and, no doubt, particularly the slave States.
When they come as invaders, with arms in their hands, and address to their kindred and their race, who are enslaved by us,
words of passion and hate and vengeance, and put arms into their
hands, it will be like letting the young tiger taste of blood. When
he gets the taste, his savage fury will soon know no bounds, and
he will glut every infernal passion.

Sir, I am acquainted with the negro race. I have been born in the same family with them. I have grown up with them. I have played with them. They have shared with me my joys and my sorrows. I have shared with them theirs. I own slaves now. Next to my wife and my children, I would defend my slaves, and would guard them from every wrong; and that is the universal sentiment of the slaveholders in my State. I wish you would come among us and see the institution there. My slaves are not for sale. There is no money that would buy my faithful and contented slaves; and they are all so, so far as I know. I have not seen a slave chastised for twenty years; and it is a rare occurrence that you hear of it in my State. They are clothed well, they are fed well, they are housed well, they have every attention of the most skillful physicians that the members of the white family have. Yes, and in the midst of cholera and pestilence and death, their owners stand by them and share the malaria and the infection with them. I have seen it done again and again. If it was not egotism, I would say that I have performed that part myself, without any regard to consequences or the peril of my life, and I would do it forever.

The perpetual agitation of the slave question is what has brought on this rebellion. I admit that slavery has been one of the causes; a remote cause, but a pretty powerful one. The cotton States, by their slave labor, have become wealthy, and many of their planters have princely revenues—from $50,000 to $100,000 a year. This wealth has begot pride and insolence and ambition, and these points of the Southern character have been displayed most insultingly in the halls of Congress. I admit it all. But in these Southern States, and among these planters, are some of the truest gentlemen, in the highest sense of the word, that I have ever known, and some of the purest patriots. I admit, however, that, as a class, the wealthy cotton-growers are insolent; they are proud; they are domineering; they are ambitious. They have monopolized the Government in its honors for forty or fifty years, with few interruptions. When they saw the scepter about to depart from them in the election of Lincoln, sooner than give up office, and the spoils of office, in their mad and wicked ambition they determined to disrupt the old Confederation and to erect a new one, where they would have undisputed power. I am for meeting them in that unholy purpose of theirs. I want them met in battle array. Whenever they send an army in the field, I want that army met and overthrown.

They had some reason to complain of a few old women and fanatical preachers and madmen in the Northern States, who were always agitating this question; but nine out of ten of the Northern people were sound upon the subject. They were opposed to the extension of slavery, and I do not condemn them for that; but they were willing to accord to the slaveholder and to the slave States all their constitutional rights.

I think that the last Congress made a great mistake in not accepting Mr. Crittenden's compromise. It would have left the cotton States without a pretext by which they could have deluded and misled the masses of the people. The last letter that Old Hickory wrote—and there is a gentleman now in this body who has it in his possession—said that the tariff was only a pretext for the disturbance in the form of nullification in 1832–'33; that they meditated treason and a separate Southern empire or confederation; that they only seized that as the pretext for making their outbreak, and that they would next seize upon the slave question as another pretext. They have done so.

Mr. President, both sides have sinned, North and South, the extreme men. I could live by these gentlemen who surround me as neighbors, holding my slaves, and they opposed to the institution. I would do it in the most perfect security, and they would do it without infringing on any of my rights. I know they would; but it is not so with the extreme men; I am afraid it is not so with the gentleman from Massachusetts, to whom I have been addressing some of my remarks. I would fain hope it was so, and I shall rejoice to find that I am mistaken. But what say some of these extreme Northern men about slavery and about the Constitution? Here is what one says:

"The Constitution is a covenant with death and an agreement with hell."—*The Liberator*.
" No union with slaveholders."—*Ibid*.

There is proscription, without condition, inexorable and forever. " No union with slaveholders." It is that fanatical sentiment that has brought many of them to curse and to execrate the memory of Washington, as well as of the Constitution. Here is what another of them has said:

" The anti-slavery party had hoped for and planned disunion because it would lead to the development of mankind and the elevation of the black man."—*Wendell Phillips*.

Phillips gives his sympathies, as the gentleman from Indiana gives his, to the Southern confederation, and he says "the South deserved to succeed because she had exhibited better statesmanship and more capacity for control." The Abolitionists subscribe to a memorial to Congress that contains this prayer:

"That amid the varied events which are constantly occurring, and which will more and more occur during the momentous struggle in which we are engaged, such measures may be adopted as will insure emancipation."

That is the great end and object for which many of these fanatics contend; it is not the re-establishment of the Constitution. I want the Constitution re-established as Washington made it. In attempting to put down this rebellion and to prevent a revolution, I do not want Congress itself to inaugurate and consummate a revolution. No, Mr. President, let Congress do its duty in this war faithfully, fearlessly. The people are doing theirs; they have come up to the rescue of the imperiled capital and Government as no people ever came up before. Yea, from the east to the west, especially in the free States, they are as one man. Kentucky has been invaded. The Confederate government has avowed that it will have Kentucky and Maryland and Missouri. They proclaimed, when they invaded Kentucky, that Kentucky was necessary to the Southern confederation, and they would have it at the cost of blood and of conquest. I am for meeting them, not only with sword, but with sword and shield, and I am for fighting them to extermination until we beat them back, having profaned so outrageously our soil. Our brothers of the northwestern States, and of the extreme northwestern States, have come to our rescue with a generosity and a devotion and a brotherhood that fill ns with admiration and gratitude. Never, oh! never were there more welcome visitants to any country. They have seen us; they have seen our institutions; we have seen them; we have become better acquainted with each other, and we have learned to esteem each other more truthfully and correctly. They are beginning to marry our daughters, and we will send our sons to marry their daughters, and let us establish a union of hearts and a union of hands that will last forever.

Why, Mr. President, Kentucky has almost peopled the northwestern States, especially Indiana and Illinois. I have no doubt that one fourth of the people of Indiana are either native-born Kentuckians or the sons and daughters of native-born Kentuckians. They are bone of our bone and flesh of our flesh. When you offer to the Union men of Kentucky the choice, whether they will remain united forever with Indiana and Ohio and Illinois, or go with Georgia and South Carolina and Florida, they will answer,

" A thousand fold will we be united rather with the Northwest than with those distant States.

They have proved their truth to the Union; they have proved their sympathy and their kindred to us. When they were young, Kentucky sent forth its chivalry, and shed its blood in their defense. In Harmer's and St. Clair's campaigns the unbroken wilderness was made red with the best blood of Kentucky. At Tippecanoe, in 1811, Indiana received from Kentucky the same oblation. In the war of 1812, Ohio, Indiana, and Michigan all had Kentucky blood poured out as water to drive the savage foe, both British and Indian, from their borders; and never, never was there a call upon Kentucky, that her true and brave sons did not go to the defense of their common country in these sister States. We felt that these States owed us something; but oh! how nobly and truthfully and fully are they paying the debt. I have seen mothers and daughters, fathers and sons—the whole population assembled all through my portion of Kentucky to meet and to greet these coming hosts from Ohio and Indiana, to protect their Government, and to protect that State which had protected them in bygone days. And oh! what meetings they were, what an outpouring of the heart and of all its truest and best sympathies! I have been in their camps, I have mingled with their officers, I have conversed with their soldiers, I have addressed their regiments; they have elected me honorary member of their regiments. I know your Cills and your Nortons, your Harrises, your Heckers, foreigners and natives, who are commanders of these regiments. I know that they have as nine to one expressed to me that their purpose, and their only purpose in waging this war, was the restoration of the Union and the vindication of the Government, and not to war upon slavery. Thus writes one of them from the camp at Glenn's Fork, Pulaski County, and no doubt this gallant son of Indiana was in the late hard-fought battle there.

" As an Indianian, and a member of the army of the Union, I can not fail to express my satisfaction at the just and conservative course of the Louisville *Journal* on the slavery question. Indiana is not fighting for the emancipation of the slaves, but for the restoration of law and order. When that shall have been accomplished, our mission is ended.

" Out of the officers and soldiers of the Tenth Indiana, I do not know of one Abolitionist. If Congress would legislate for the benefit of *white men*, and let the negro alone, it would be better."

And oh! how much better it would be! That is the instinct of truth and patriotism, of mind and heart; and that utterance nine tenths of the soldiery of the Northwest speak and will speak forever. If, sir, you had proposed your measure before this grand and all-conquering army had been collected together, and told them it was to be a war upon slavery, you would never have had one fourth of the host in the field that you have. When a party wins power, the best way to preserve it is to use it in moderation, and especially within the Constitution. Fanaticism and passion and excitement never did and never will wisely legislate for or govern any country. Senators, you are supposed to act, not from passion and a desire of vengeance and to punish, but from reason and patriotism, and right and truth, and eternal justice. If you act upon these principles, and allay the swelling passions as they rise in your bosoms, I am not afraid to trust you.

But, Mr. President, these fanatics, these political and social demons—your Greeleys, your Cheevers, your Phillipses, and your Garrisons—that come here, like spirits from the infernal regions, to bring another pandemonium into our councils, to violate the Constitution, to walk to the destruction of slavery over all its broken fragments, and to oppose Lincoln, as honest and as pure a man as lives, because he does not go with them in their extreme opposition to slavery—what ought to be done with them? The utterances which I have read to you they have dared to give in this city. They have desecrated the Smithsonian Institution to the utterance of such sentiments. If secessionists or those who sympathize with them had made the same utterances, they would have been sent, and properly sent, to Fort Lafayette or to Fort Warren. What should you do with these monsters? I will tell you what I would do with them; that horrid monster, Greeley, and those other monsters, who are howling over this city like famished wolves after slavery—that slavery which was established by the Constitution and by Washington. What should be done with them? If I had the power, I would take them with the worst "secesh," and I would hang them in pairs. [Sensation.] I wish before God that I could inflict that punishment upon them. It would not be too severe. They are the agitators; they are disunionists; they are the madmen who are willing to call up all the infernal passions and all the horrors of servile war, and to disregard utterly the Constitution, and march triumphantly over its broken, disjected fragments to attain their unholy purposes, and I am too fearful that the honorable gentleman from Massachusetts sympathizes with them.

Mr. President, I most humbly ask the pardon of the Senate for this desultory, lengthy, and discursive discourse. I trust I have wounded the feelings of no gentleman. It was not my purpose to do so; it was far from my purpose. I want the Union restored. If it is to be restored, it is by the instrumentality of the President of the United States. In his integrity and patriotism and truth I place implicit confidence. He is a moderate man in his principles. He is a just man. He is a wise man. If he were left to his own counsels, to the suggestions of his own reason, to the impulses of his own heart, if he had a little more of the stern and iron element of a Clay or an "Old Hickory," and would act out his own will, and repress the men whose pestilent counsels distract him and neutralize his efforts to bring this war to a speedy and to a triumphant close, I think that he would act his part more nobly and with more success. So far as I am concerned, he has my confidence and my respect. I can clothe him with no power by my vote to carry on this war vigorously and successfully, within the Constitution, that I will withhold from him. I want the aid of Black Republicans and Republicans and Democrats and all, in this holy work. I care not what laurels and honors and hopes of future emolument and office any man may win.

I admired, beyond measure almost, the dead hero Lyon. In my judgment, he showed himself more of a warrior than any man who has yet exhibited himself in the field during this struggle. The moment that he detected the purposes of Camp Jackson at St. Louis, he moved upon it and captured it and all of its hosts. When the traitor Jackson, the disloyal governor of Missouri, issued his treasonable proclamation, and fled toward Booneville, the active, the dauntless, and the military Lyon was after him with his army, and overtook and dispersed his hosts to the wind. He and Sigel, a foreigner, but a warrior, himself a man of military education, a genius naturally, met the foe at Carthage, and fought a small battle, but one of the most perfect battles, in my judgment, of which history gives any record. Then the enemy returned in a vast host to Springfield. With an inferior army, Lyon and Sigel met them again. Two regiments were at Rolla that ought to have been sent to reinforce them, but they were not sent; if they had been, our arms might have won the day. Lyon, to save the cause of his country and of Missouri, made the battle. He rushed into the thickest of the fight, and he fell a voluntary martyr to his country's cause, and then Sigel made one of the most masterly retreats that I have read of. I wish that that dead hero was now alive, again to marshal our armies to victory and to help to deliver the country from its imperiled condition. Mr. President, let any warrior come who has capacity to bring it to a close or to contribute materially to its success, I care not what his politics, I give him my faith, my support, my admiration, my gratitude, and so will my State, or the Union portion of it. We want the assistance of everybody, of every Union man to bring this war to a close, and we trusted, before I left home, and I still trust, that these discordant questions, these measures which must divide us, will be left unattempted, at least until the war has crushed out the most wicked and infamous rebellion that ever was made in the tide of time.

AFRICAN SLAVERY,

THE CORNER-STONE OF THE SOUTHERN CONFEDERACY.

A Speech by Hon. Alexander H. Stephens, Vice-President of the Confederate States of America, delivered at the Atheneum, Savannah, March 22, 1861.

The Mayor, who presided, introduced the speaker with a few pertinent remarks, and Mr. Stephens was greeted with deafening rounds of applause, after which he spoke as follows:

Mr. Mayor and Gentlemen of the Committee, and Fellow-Citizens—For this reception, you will please accept my most profound and sincere thanks. The compliment is doubtless intended as much, or more perhaps, in honor of the occasion, and my public position in connection with the great events now crowding upon us, than to me personally and individually. It is, however, none the less appreciated on that account. We are in the midst of one of the greatest epochs in our history. The last ninety days will mark one of the most memorable eras in the history of modern civilization.

[There was a general call from the outside of the building for the speaker to go out; that there were more outside than in. The Mayor rose and requested silence at the doors; said Mr. Stephens's health would not permit him to speak in the open air. Mr. Stephens said he would leave it to the audience whether he should proceed indoors or out. There was a general cry indoors, as the ladies—a large number of whom were present—could not hear outside. Mr. Stephens said that the accommodation of the ladies would determine the question, and he would proceed where he was. At this point the uproar and clamor outside were greater still for the speaker to go out on the steps. This was quieted by Col. Lawton, Col. Foreman, Judge Jackson, and Mr. J. W. Owens, going out and stating the facts of the case to the dense mass of men, women, and children who were outside, and entertaining them in short, brief speeches, Mr. Stephens all this time quietly sitting down until the furor subsided.]

Mr. Stephens rose and said—When perfect quiet is restored I shall proceed. I can not speak as long as there is any noise or confusion. I shall take my time. I feel as though I could spend the night with you, if necessary. [Loud applause.] I very much regret that every one who desires can not hear what I have to say, not that I have any display to make, or anything very entertaining to present; but such views as I have to give I wish all, not only in this city, but in this State, and throughout our Confederated Republic, could hear, who have a desire to hear them.

I was remarking that we were passing through one of the greatest revolutions in the annals of the world. Seven States have, within the last three months, thrown off an old government, and formed a new. This revolution has been signally marked, up to this time, by the fact of its having been accomplished without the loss of a single drop of blood. [Applause.] This new constitution, or form of government, constitutes the subject to which your attention will be partly invited.

In reference to it, I make this first general remark: It amply secures all our ancient rights, franchises, and privileges. All the great principles of Magna Charta are retained in it. No citizen is deprived of life, liberty, or property but by the judgment of his peers, under the laws of the land. The great principle of religious liberty, which was the honor and pride of the old Constitution, is still maintained and secured. All the essentials of the old Constitution, which have endeared it to the hearts of the American people, have been preserved and perpetuated. [Applause.] Some changes have been made; of these I shall speak presently. Some of these I should have preferred not to have been made, but these perhaps meet the cordial approbation of a majority of this audience, if not an overwhelming majority of the people of the Confederacy. Of them, therefore, I will not speak. But other important changes do meet my cordial approbation. They form great improvements on the old Constitution. So, taking the whole new Constitution, I have no hesitancy in giving it as my judgment that it is decidedly better than the old. [Applause.] Allow me briefly to allude to some of these improvements. The question of building up class interests, or fostering one branch of industry to the prejudice of another, under the exercise of the revenue power, which gave us so much trouble under the old Constitution, is put at rest forever under the new. We allow the imposition of no duty with a view of giving advantages to one class of persons, in any trade or business, over those of another. All, under our system, stand upon the same broad principles of perfect equality. Honest labor and enterprise are left free and unrestricted in whatever pursuit they may be engaged. This subject came well nigh causing a rupture of the old Union, under the lead of the gallant Palmetto State, which lies on our border, in 1833.

This old thorn of the tariff, which occasioned the cause of so much irritation in the old body politic, is removed forever from the new. [Applause.] Again, the subject of internal improvements, under the power of Congress to regulate commerce, is put at rest under our system. The power claimed by construction under the old Constitution was, at least, a doubtful one—it rested solely upon construction. We, of the South, generally apart from considerations of constitutional principles, opposed its exercise upon grounds of expediency and justice. Notwithstanding this opposition, millions of money in the common Treasury had been drawn for such purposes. Our opposition sprung from no hostility to commerce, or all necessary aids for facilitating it. With us it was simply a question upon *whom* the burden should fall. In Georgia, for instance, we had done as much for the cause of internal improvements as any other portion of the country, according to population and means. We have stretched out lines of railroads from the seaboard to the mountains; dug down the hills and filled up the valleys at a cost of not less than $25,000,000. All this was done to open up an outlet for our products of the interior, and those to the west of us, to reach the marts of the world. No State was in greater need of such facilities than Georgia, but we had not asked that these works should be made by appropriations out of the common Treasury. The cost of the grading, the superstructure, and equipments of our roads was borne by those who entered upon the enterprise. Nay, more, not only the cost of the iron, no small item in the aggregate cost, was borne in the same way, but we were compelled to pay into the common Treasury several millions of dollars for the privilege of importing the iron after the price was paid for it abroad. What justice was there in taking this money, which our people paid into the common Treasury on the importation of our iron, and applying it to the improvement of rivers and harbors elsewhere?

The true principle is, to subject commerce of every locality to whatever burdens may be necessary to facilitate it. If Charleston harbor needs improvement, let the commerce of Charleston bear the burden. If the mouth of the Savannah River has to be cleared out, let the sea-going navigation which is benefited by it bear the burden. So with the mouths of the Alabama and Mississippi rivers. Just as the products of the interior, our cotton, wheat, corn, and other articles have to bear the necessary rates of freight over our railroads to reach the seas. This is again the broad principle of perfect equality and justice. [Applause.] And it is specially held forth and established in our new Constitution.

Another feature to which I will allude is, that the new Constitution provides that cabinet ministers and heads of departments shall have the privilege of seats upon the floor of the Senate and House of Representatives—shall have the right to participate in the debates and discussions upon the various subjects of administration. I should have preferred that this provision should have gone farther, and allowed the President to select his constitutional advisers from the Senate and House of Representatives. . That would have conformed entirely to the practice in the British Parliament, which, in my judgment, is one of the wisest provisions in the British Parliament. It is the only feature that saves that government. It is that which gives it stability in its facility to change its administration. Ours, as it is, is a great approximation to the right principle.

Under the old Constitution a secretary of the Treasury, for instance, had no opportunity, save by his annual reports, of presenting any scheme or plan of finance or other matter. He had no opportunity of explaining, expounding, enforcing, or defending his views of policy; his only resort was through the medium of an organ. In the British Parliament the premier brings in his budget, and stands before the nation responsible for its every item. If it is indefensible, he falls before the attacks upon it, as he ought to. This will now be the case to a limited extent under our system. Our heads of departments can speak for themselves and the administration, in behalf of its entire policy, without resorting to the indirect and highly objectionable medium of a newspaper. It is to be greatly hoped that under our system we shall never have what is known as a government organ. [Rapturous applause.]

[A noise again arose from the clamor of the crowd outside, who wished to hear Mr. Stephens, and for some moments interrupted him. The Mayor rose and called on the police to preserve order. Quiet being restored, Mr. S. proceeded.]

Another change in the Constitution relates to the length of the tenure of the Presidential office. In the new Constitution it is six years instead of four, and the President rendered ineligible for re-election. This is certainly a decidedly conservative change. It will remove from the incumbent all temptation to use his office or exert the powers confided to him for any objects of personal ambition. The only incentive to that higher ambition which should move and actuate one holding such high trusts in his hands will be the good of the people, the advancement, prosperity, happiness, safety, honor, and true glory of the Confederacy. [Applause.]

But not to be tedious in enumerating the numerous changes for the better, allow me to allude to one other—though last, not least : The new Constitution has put at rest, *forever*, all agitating questions relating to our peculiar institution—African slavery as it exists among us—the proper *status* of the negro in our form of civilization. This was the immediate cause of the late rupture and present revolution. Jefferson, in his forecast, had anticipated this, as the "rock upon which the old Union would split." He was right. What was conjecture with him is now a realized fact. But whether he fully comprehended the great truth upon which that rock *stood* and *stands*, may be doubted. The prevailing ideas entertained by him and most of the leading statesmen at the time of the formation of the old Constitution were, that the enslavement of the African was in violation of the laws of nature; that it was wrong in *principle*, socially, morally, and politically. It was an evil they knew not well how to deal with, but the general opinion of the men of that day was that, somehow or other, in the order of Providence, the institution would be evanescent and pass away. This idea, though not incorporated in the Constitution, was the prevailing idea at the time. The Constitution, it is true, secured every essential guaranty to the institution while it should last, and hence no argument can be justly used against the constitutional guaranties thus secured, because of the common sentiment of the day. Those ideas, however, were fundamentally wrong. They rested upon the assumption of the equality of races. This was an error. It was a sandy foundation, and the idea of a government built upon it; when the "storm came and the wind blew, it *fell*."

Our new government is founded upon exactly the opposite idea; its foundations are laid, its corner-stone rests upon the great truth that the negro is not equal to the white man. That slavery—subordination to the superior race—is his natural and moral condition. [Applause.]

This, our new government, is the first in the history of the world based upon this great physical, philosophical, and moral truth. This truth has been slow in the process of its development, like all other truths in the various departments of science. It has been so even among us. Many who hear me, perhaps, can recollect well that this truth was not generally admitted even within their day. The errors of the past generation still clung to many as late as twenty years ago. Those at the North who still cling to these errors, with a zeal above knowledge, we justly denominate fanatics. All fanaticism springs from an aberration of the mind—from a defect in reasoning. It is a species of insanity. One of the most striking characteristics of insanity, in many instances, is forming correct conclusions from fancied or erroneous premises; so with the anti-slavery fanatics; their conclusions are right, if their premises are. They assume that the negro is equal, and hence conclude that he is entitled to equal privileges and rights with the white man. If their premise were correct, their conclusion would be logical and just; but their premise being wrong, their whole argument fails. I recollect once of having heard a gentleman from one of the Northern States, of great power and ability, announce in the House of Representatives, with imposing effect, that we of the South would be compelled, ultimately, to yield upon this subject of slavery; that it was as impossible to war successfully against a principle in politics, as it was in physics or mechanics. That the principle would ultimately prevail. That we, in maintaining slavery as it exists with us, were warring against a principle, a principle founded in nature, the principle of the equality of man. The reply I made to him was, that upon his own grounds we should succeed, and that he and his associates in their crusades against our institutions, would ultimately fail. The truth announced that it was as impossible to war successfully against a principle in politics as in physics and mechanics, I admitted, but told him that it was he and those acting with him who were warring against a principle. They were attempting to make things equal which the Creator had made unequal.

In the conflict thus far, success has been on our side, complete throughout the length and breadth of the Confederate States. It is upon this, as I have stated, our social fabric is firmly planted, and I can not permit myself to doubt the ultimate success of a full recognition of this principle throughout the civilized and enlightened world.

As I have stated, the truth of this principle may be slow in development, as all truths are, and ever have been, in the various branches of science. It was so with the principles announced by Galileo; it was so with Adam Smith and his principles of political economy. It was so with Harvey and his theory of the circulation of the blood. It is stated that not a single one of the medical profession, living at the time of the announcement of the truths made by him, admitted them. Now, they are universally acknowledged. May we not, therefore, look with confidence to the ultimate universal acknowledgment of the truths upon which our system rests? It is the first government ever instituted upon principles in strict conformity to nature, and the ordination of Providence, in furnishing the materials of human society. Many governments have been founded upon the principle of the enslavement of certain classes; but the classes thus enslaved were of the same race and in violation of the laws of nature. Our system commits no such violation of nature's laws. The negro by nature, or by the curse against Canaan, is fitted for that condition which he occupies in our system. The architect, in the construction of buildings, lays the foundation with proper materials—the granite—then comes the brick or the marble. The substratum of our society is made of the material fitted by nature for it, and by experience we know that it is best not only for the superior, but for the inferior race that it should be so. It is, indeed, in conformity with the ordinance of the Creator. It is not for us to inquire into the wisdom of His ordinances or to question them. For His own purposes He has made one race to differ from another, as He has made "one star to differ from another in glory."

The great objects of humanity are best attained, when conformed to His laws and decrees, in the formation of governments as well as in all things else. Our Confederacy is founded upon principles in strict conformity with these laws. This stone which was rejected by the first builders, "is become the chief stone of the corner" in our new edifice. [Applause.]

I have been asked, what of the future? It has been appre-
hended by some that we would have arrayed against us the civilized world. I care not who or how many they may be, when we
stand upon the eternal principles of truth we are obliged and must
triumph. [Immense applause.]

Thousands of people who begin to understand these truths are
not yet completely out of the shell. They do not see them in their
length and breadth. We hear much of the civilization and Chris-
tianization of the barbarous tribes of Africa. In my judgment,
those ends will never be attained, but by first teaching them the
lesson taught to Adam, that "in the sweat of thy brow shalt thou
eat bread" [applause], and teaching them to work, and feed, and
clothe themselves. But to pass on: some have propounded the
inquiry, whether it is practicable for us to go on with the Confederacy without further accessions? Have we the means and
ability to maintain nationality among the powers of the earth?
On this point I would barely say, that as anxiously as we all have
been and are for the Border States, with institutions similar with
ours, to join us, still we are abundantly able to maintain our position, even if they should ultimately make up their minds not to
cast their destiny with ours. That they ultimately will join us—
be compelled to do it—is my confident belief, but we can get on
very well without them, even if they should not.

We have all the essential elements of a high national career.
The idea has been given out at the North, and even in the Border
States, that we are too small and too weak to maintain a separate
nationality. This is a great mistake. In extent of territory we
embrace 564,000 square miles and upward. This is upward of
200,000 square miles more than was included within the limits of
the original thirteen States. It is an area of country more than
double the territory of France or the Austrian Empire. France,
in round numbers, has but 212,000 square miles. Austria, in
round numbers, has 248,000 square miles. Ours is greater than
both combined. It is greater than all France, Spain, Portugal, and
Great Britain, including England, Ireland, and Scotland together.
In population we have upward of eight millions, according to the
census of 1860; this includes white and black. The entire population, including white and black, of the original thirteen States,
was less than 4,000,000 in 1790, and still less in '76, when the independence of our fathers was achieved. If they, with a less population, dared maintain their independence against the greatest

power on earth, shall we have any apprehension of maintaining ours now?

In point of material wealth and resources we are greatly in advance of them. The taxable property of the Confederate States can not be less than $22,000,000,000. This, I think, I venture but little in saying, may be considered as five times more than the colonies possessed at the time they achieved their independence. Georgia alone possessed last year, according to the report of our Controller-General, $672,000,000 of taxable property. The debts of the seven Confederate States sum up, in the aggregate, less than $18,000,000; while the existing debts of the other of the late United States sum up, in the aggregate, the enormous amount of $174,000,000. This is without taking into the account the heavy city debts, corporation debts, and railroad debts, which press, and will continue to press, a heavy incubus upon the resources of those States. These debts, added to others, make a sum total not much under $500,000,000. With such an area of territory—with such an amount of population—with a climate and soil unsurpassed by any on the face of the earth—with such resources already at our command—with productions which control the commerce of the world, who can entertain any apprehensions as to our success, whether others join us or not?

It is true, I believe, I state but the common sentiment, when I declare my earnest desire that the Border States should join us. The differences of opinion that existed among us anterior to secession related more to the policy in securing that result by co-operation than from any difference upon the ultimate security we all looked to in common.

These differences of opinion were more in reference to policy than principle, and as Mr. Jefferson said in his inaugural, in 1801, after the heated contest preceding his election, there might be differences in opinion without differences in principle, and that all, to some extent, had been Federalists and all Republicans; so it may now be said of us, that whatever differences of opinion as to the best policy in having a co-operation with our border sister Slave States, if the worst come to the worst, that as we were all co-operationists, we are now all for independence, whether they come or not. [Continued applause.]

In this connection I take this occasion to state that I was not without grave and serious apprehension, that if the worst came to the worst, and cutting loose from the old government would be the only remedy for our safety and security, it would be attended with much more serious ills than it has been as yet. Thus far we have seen none of those incidents which usually attend revolutions. No such material as such convulsions usually throw up has been seen. Wisdom, prudence, and patriotism have marked every step of our progress thus far. This augurs well for the future, and it is a matter of sincere gratification to me, that I am enabled to make the declaration of the men I met in the Congress at Montgomery (I may be pardoned for saying this), an abler, wiser—a more conservative, deliberate, determined, resolute, and patriotic body of men I never met in my life. [Great applause.] Their works speak for them; the Provisional Government speaks for them; the Constitution of the permanent Government will be a lasting monument of their worth, merit, and statesmanship. [Applause.]

But to return to the question of the future. What is to be the result of this revolution?

Will everything, commenced so well, continue as it has begun? In reply to this anxious inquiry, I can only say it all depends upon ourselves. A young man starting out in life on his majority, with health, talent, and ability, under a favoring Providence, may be said to be the architect of his own fortunes. His destinies are in his own hands. He may make for himself a name of honor or dishonor, according to his own acts. If he plants himself upon truth, integrity, honor, and uprightness, with industry, patience, and energy, he can not fail of success. So it is with us; we are a young Republic, just entering upon the arena of nations; we will be the architect of our own fortunes. Our destiny, under Providence, is in our own hands. With wisdom, prudence, and statesmanship on the part of our public men, and intelligence, virtue, and patriotism on the part of the people, success, to the full measures of our most sanguine hopes, may be looked for. But if we become divided—if schisms arise—if dissensions spring up—if factions are engendered—if party spirit, nourished by unholy personal ambition, shall rear its hydra head, I have no good to prophesy for you. Without intelligence, virtue, integrity, and patriotism on the part of the people, no republic or representative government can be durable or stable.

We have intelligence, and virtue, and patriotism. All that is required is to cultivate and perpetuate these. Intelligence will not do without virtue. France was a nation of philosophers. These philosophers became Jacobins. They lacked that virtue, that devotion to moral principle, and that patriotism which is essential to good government. Organized upon principles of perfect justice and right—seeking amity and friendship with all other powers—I see no obstacle in the way of our upward and onward progress. Our growth, by accessions from other States, will depend greatly upon whether we present to the world, as I trust we shall, a better government than that to which they belong. If we do this, North Carolina, Tennessee, and Arkansas can not hesitate long; neither can Virginia, Kentucky, and Missouri. They will necessarily gravitate to us by an imperious law. We made ample provision in our Constitution for the admission of other States; it is more guarded, and wisely so, I think, than the old Constitution on the same subject, but not too guarded to receive them as fast as it may be proper. Looking to the distant future, and, perhaps, not very distant either, it is not beyond the range of possibility, and even probability, that all the great States of the Northwest shall gravitate this way as well as Tennessee, Kentucky, Missouri, Arkansas, etc. Should they do so, our doors are wide enough to receive them, but not until they are ready to assimilate with us in principle.

The process of disintegration in the old Union may be expected to go on with almost absolute certainty. We are now the nucleus of a growing power, which, if we are true to ourselves, our destiny, and high mission, will become the controlling power on this continent. To what extent accession will go on in the process of time, or where it will end, the future will determine. So far as it concerns States of the old Union, they will be upon no such principle of *reconstruction* as now spoken of, but upon *reorganization* and new assimilation. [Loud applause.] Such are some of the glimpses of the future as I catch them.

But at first we must necessarily meet with the inconveniences, and difficulties, and embarrassments incident to all changes of government. These will be felt in our postal affairs and changes in the channel of trade. These inconveniences, it is to be hoped, will be but temporary, and must be borne with patience and forbearance.

As to whether we shall have war with our late confederates, or whether all matters of differences between us shall be amicably settled, I can only say that the prospect for a peaceful adjustment is better, so far as I am informed, than it has been.

The prospect of war is at least not so threatening as it has been.

The idea of coercion shadowed forth in President Lincoln's Inaugural seems not to be followed up thus far so vigorously as was expected. Fort Sumter, it is believed, will soon be evacuated. What course will be pursued toward Fort Pickens and the other forts on the Gulf, is not so well understood. It is to be greatly desired that all of them should be surrendered. Our object is *Peace*, not only with the North, but with the world. All matters relating to the public property, public liabilities of the Union when we were members of it, we are ready and willing to adjust and settle, upon the principles of right, equality and good faith. War can be of no more benefit to the North than to us. The idea of coercing us, or subjugating us, is utterly preposterous. Whether the intention of evacuating Fort Sumter is to be received as an evidence of a desire for a peaceful solution of our difficulties with the United States, or the result of necessity, I will not undertake to say. I would fain hope the former. Rumors are afloat, however, that it is the result of necessity. All I can say to you, therefore, on that point is, keep your armor bright and your powder dry. [Enthusiastic applause.]

The surest way to secure peace is to show your ability to maintain your rights. The principles and position of the present Administration of the United States—the Republican party—present some puzzling questions. While it is a fixed principle with them never to allow the increase of a foot of slave territory, they seem to be equally determined not to part with an inch "of the accursed soil." Notwithstanding their clamor against the institution, they seem to be equally opposed to getting more, or letting go what they have got. They were ready to fight on the accession of Texas, and are equally ready to fight now on her secession. Why is this? How can this strange paradox be accounted for? There seems to be but one rational solution, and that is, notwithstanding their professions of humanity, they are disinclined to give up the benefits they derive from slave labor. Their philanthropy yields to their interest. The idea of enforcing the laws has but one object, and that is a collection of the taxes raised by slave labor to swell the fund necessary to meet their heavy appropriations. The spoils is what they are after, though they come from the labor of the slave. [Continued applause.]

Mr. Stephens reviewed at some length the extravagance and profligacy of appropriations by the Congress of the United States for several years past, and in this connection took occasion to allude to another one of the great improvements in our new Constitution, which is a clause prohibiting Congress from appropriating any money from the Treasury except by a two-thirds vote, unless it be for some object which the Executive may say is necessary to carry on the Government.

When it is thus asked for and estimated, he continued, the majority may appropriate. This was a new feature.

Our fathers had guarded the assessment of taxes by insisting that representation and taxation should go together. This was inherited from the mother country—England. It was one of the principles upon which the Revolution had been fought. Our fathers also provided in the old Constitution that all appropriation bills should originate in the Representative branch of Congress; but our new Constitution went a step further, and guarded not only the pockets of the people, but also the public money, after it was taken from their pockets.

He alluded to the difficulties and embarrassments which seemed to surround the question of a peaceful solution of the controversy with the old Government. How can it be done? is perplexing many minds. The President seems to think that he can not recognize our independence, nor can he, with and by the advice of the Senate, do so. The Constitution makes no such provision. A general convention of all the States has been suggested by some. Without proposing to solve the difficulty, he barely made the following suggestions:

That as the admission of States by Congress under the Constitution was an act of legislation, and in the nature of a contract or compact between the States admitted and the others admitting, why should not this contract or compact be regarded as of like character with all other civil contracts—liable to be rescinded by mutual agreement of both parties? The seceding States have rescinded it on their part. Why can not the whole question be settled, if the North desire peace, simply by the Congress, in both branches, with the concurrence of the President, giving their consent to the separation, and a recognition of our independence? This he merely offered as a suggestion, as one of the ways in which it might be done with much less violence to constructions of the Constitution than many other acts of that Government. [Applause.] The difficulty has to be solved in some way or other—this may be regarded as a fixed fact.

Several other points were alluded to by Mr. S., particularly as to the policy of the new Government toward foreign nations and our commercial relations with them. Free trade, as far as practicable, would be the policy of this Government. No higher duties would be imposed on foreign importation than would be necessary to support the Government upon the strictest economy.

In olden times the olive branch was considered the emblem of peace. We will send to the nations of the earth another and far more potential emblem of the same—the COTTON PLANT. The present duties were levied with a view of meeting the present necessities and exigencies, in preparation for war, if need be; but if we had peace—and he hoped we might—and trade should resume its proper course, a duty of ten per cent. upon foreign importations, it was thought, might be sufficient to meet the expenditures of the Government. If some articles should be left on the free list, as they now are, such as breadstuffs, etc., then, of course, duties upon others would have to be higher—but in no event to an extent to embarrass trade and commerce. He concluded in an earnest appeal for union and harmony, on the part of all the people, in support of the common cause, in which we are all enlisted, and upon the issues of which such great consequences depend.

If, said he, we are true to ourselves, true to our cause, true to our destiny, true to our high mission, in presenting to the world the highest type of civilization ever exhibited by man, there will be found in our lexicon no such word as Fail.

Mr. Stephens took his seat amid a burst of enthusiasm and applause such as the Atheneum has never displayed within its walls within "the recollection of the oldest inhabitant."

www.ingramcontent.com/pod-product-compliance
Lightning Source LLC
Chambersburg PA
CBHW031809090426
42739CB00008B/1228